ON THE HUNT WITH
HYENAS

BY JODY JENSEN SHAFFER

Published by The Child's World®
1980 Lookout Drive • Mankato, MN 56003-1705
800-599-READ • www.childsworld.com

Acknowledgments
The Child's World®: Mary Berendes, Publishing Director
Red Line Editorial: Design, editorial direction, and production
Photographs ©: Shutterstock Images, cover, 1, 4, 7, 13, 16, 21; Stephanie
Periquet/Shutterstock Images, 6; iStockphoto, 8, 11; Red Line Editorial, 10;
Mike Dexter/Shutterstock Images, 12; Jez Bennett/Shutterstock Images,
14; Bridgena Barnard/Shutterstock Images, 17; Dave Pusey/Shutterstock
Images, 18

ISBN 9781634074537

LCCN 2015946214

Printed in the United States of America
Mankato, MN
December, 2015
PA02279

TABLE OF
CONTENTS

Chapter 1

THE HUNT

I t is night on the savanna. The scorching sun has set. The temperature has cooled. Trees dot the plains. But the trees give little shade during the heat of the day. Spotted hyenas sleep in the long grass when the sun is hot. But now the moon is shining. A group of hyenas, called a hyena clan, is restless and hungry. The **alpha female** is in charge. This is her clan.

The alpha female stands. She stretches. She eyes a herd of zebras. They are grazing near some wildebeests. The alpha female calls to her clan. She tells them it is time to hunt. They trot toward her and stand beside their leader. A small group of five hyenas break off from the clan. Three adults, one **juvenile**, and one young cub make up their group. They will be the hunters tonight. They walk in a line behind the alpha. Most of the hunters are female. They are big and bold.

The zebras see the hyenas coming. They swish their tails and gallop back and forth. Then they run into the darkness. But the

◀ **Hyenas, especially the alpha female, are especially skilled in hunting.**

▲ **Zebras are just one kind of larger animal hyenas hunt.**

hyenas do not give up. They are patient. They follow the zebras at a walking pace. Suddenly the zebras stop. The hyenas circle them. They watch the zebras and lie down. They do it again. Circle. Watch. Lie down. They do this until they are ready to attack. Until the alpha tells them it is time.

Then the alpha female begins. She spots a large adult zebra. It has separated itself from the herd. It is around 500 pounds (227 kg). That is more than twice the alpha's size. Adult hyenas can weigh around 110 to 190 pounds (50 to 86 kg). The hyena hunters split up. They have a hunting plan. They have done this before. Two circle right. Two circle left. One heads straight for the zebra. The zebra runs and zigzags. But the hyenas are fast.

They can race up to 37 miles per hour (60 km/h). They quickly take down the zebra.

Teeth like daggers dig into the zebra's side. Sharp claws tear at its legs. The zebra falls. It can no longer run. The hunting party gathers. The rest of clan is not far behind. The alpha female eats first. She shares the kill with her cubs first. Other females and cubs eat next. The zebra is now mostly skin and bones. Low-ranking males eat last. The stragglers get only bones. It has been a successful hunt for the hyena clan.

▲ **The lower members of the hyena clan are left only bones to eat.**

Chapter 2

BUILT TO HUNT

Stomachs full, the hyena clan rests near a clump of trees. They are not picky about where they live. Hyenas live in many **habitats** in Africa. They roam woodlands, grasslands, forests, and deserts. They live near mountains and in swamp and marshy areas.

The adults quickly fall asleep. They save their energy for the next night's hunt. Hyenas are fierce **predators**. They are skilled at getting food. They are speedy and strong. And they need to be. Hunting big **prey** requires strength and speed. Hyenas can drag heavy prey using their thick, strong necks. And they can chase prey for a long time without getting tired.

Tomorrow they might hunt buffalo. Or maybe young hippos, antelopes, or foxes will cross their paths. Hyenas can even take down lions. Many animals share the hyenas' habitat, so food is all around. Hyenas will even eat wildebeest waste and plants if they must.

◄ **Hyenas' strong jaws and teeth help them rip apart their prey.**

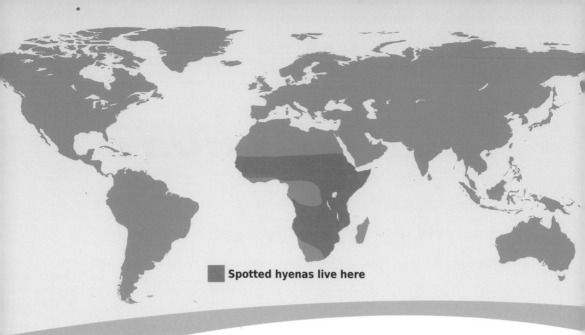

Spotted hyenas live here

▲ Spotted hyenas live only in Africa.

Sometimes hyenas are **scavengers**. They steal kills from other predators. Or they eat dead animals. Their stomachs can break down bones and skin. The only parts their stomachs cannot break down are horns, hair, and hooves. They will spit those up later.

Hyenas' thick, powerful skulls, jaws, and teeth give them an advantage over other predators. They can crunch up bone easily. Most other predators can only eat meat. But the hyenas' ability to crush and break down bone takes time. Young hyenas do not have strong jaws. They cannot crush bone. It takes many years to grow a skull and jaws that strong.

Hyenas sometimes fight vultures for dead food. ▶

▲ **Female hyenas are strong leaders.**

Mother hyenas raise their cubs for three to four years. This is much longer than other **mammals**. For cubs to survive, mothers need to give them more time to learn how to hunt. Females have to be aggressive. They have to fight off other hyenas. For many other types of mammals, males are the leaders. Not hyenas. Females also lead the clans. They are bigger and bolder than males.

◄ **Hyena cubs play with each other and their mother.**

Chapter 3

SPOTTED HYENA CLANS

The sun is now high in the sky. A hot breeze blows. Some of the hyenas in the clan wake. Mothers greet their cubs. Cubs play together. Hyenas are very social. Each clan has three to 90 hyenas. Clan size is based on **territory** size. Bigger clans control more land than small clans do.

A group of adults trot off to look after their territory. They howl. Their howl warns outsiders to stay away. Next they leave droppings. The scent of the droppings will mark their territory. The hyenas also guard their territory by walking its borders. Most clan members spend their days alone. They may wander in small groups. But an entire clan usually meets only during a kill or at the den.

Back from patrol duty, the group heads to the den. The den is the center of clan activity. Clans might have more than one den.

◄ **Hyenas stick together in clans.**

▲ **A hyena cub peeks out of the clan's den.**

It is where cubs are raised. It is also where clan members meet. Hyenas do not dig dens. They use holes and tunnels made by aardvarks or other small animals. Inside the den is cool ground. Adults rest and cubs play near the den. Cubs spend about eight months in the den with other cubs. A den can have as many as 22 cubs at one time. Adults from the clan care for all of the cubs.

The patrol group rests after its work. But it does not sleep. Hyenas are noisy. Across the savanna, a group of hyenas whoop and howl. The patrol group hears the call from 3 miles (5 km) away. The call means the clan has found their prey. The patrol group starts to cackle. It sounds like a giggle or laugh. Making as many as 11 sounds, hyenas have many ways to speak to one another.

The two groups meet up, whooping to all. They can even tell one hyena's call from another. This is just one more example of their close bond with other clan members. The alpha female steps forward to begin the hunt. The others groan and squeal to greet her.

Each hyena knows who is in charge of the clan. Clans have a clear chain of leadership. An adult female is the alpha female. She is the leader. Her female cubs will be the next alphas. Other adults and juveniles are next. Adult males have the least power in the clan. They rank below male cubs. A member with a low ranking must be smart. He must find ways to get what he needs. He may give a false cry when he wants to eat. He will make an alarm call. This call tells other hyenas to run away from danger. That way others will leave the kill, and he can eat it for himself.

▲ **Hyenas' large ears help them pick up calls from their clan members.**

Chapter 4

SPOTTED HYENA CUBS

The day draws to a close. A hunting party gathers. But one female hyena will not join them. She has been pregnant for about four months. Tonight while the others seek prey, she will give birth in a private den. Hyenas most often have two cubs. Each will weigh between 2.2 to 3.5 pounds (1.0 to 1.6 kg). They will be born with dark brown or black fur and sharp teeth. And they will start fighting with each other right away. They want to see who is more important. Sometimes the strong cub kills the weak one. After two to six weeks, the mother will move her cubs to the clan's den. Many other cubs will also be there. Each cub will know its own mother. At about two months, the cubs' hair will turn spotted brown.

The mother **nurses** her cubs for a year or more. But their mothers will start giving them meat at about five months old. If

◄ **Newborn spotted hyenas do not yet have their spots.**

the mother goes on a hunt, other adults in the clan will watch her cubs. But only the mother nurses her cubs. The cubs need to nurse every few days. Cubs learn to hunt early. When they are about one year old, they go with their mothers on hunting trips. Even with good training, many cubs do not live long. Half of them die before they are three or four years old. Most die from lion attacks. Adult females can have cubs every one to two years.

If the mother's new cubs are female, they will stay with her all their lives. If the cubs are male, they will leave the den around age three. The male cubs will join another clan. If clans get too big, an adult female will break away. She will take clan members with her. And they will form a new clan. Wild hyenas can live to be 25 years old. But tonight, the new mother is not thinking about new clans or the hunt. She is focused only on her cubs. Tonight her job is to keep her new babies safe and warm.

A cub lies down with its mother for the night. ▶

GLOSSARY

alpha female (AL-fa FEE-mail): An alpha female is a female that leads the hyena clan. Alpha females lead the hyenas in their group.

habitats (HAB-uh-tats): Habitats are places where animals and plants live naturally. Hyena habitats include Africa's woodlands, grasslands, forests, deserts, mountains, and swamp and marsh areas.

juvenile (JOO-ven-i-ell): A juvenile is a young animal. Juvenile hyenas are not yet adults.

mammals (MAM-uhlz): Mammals are warm-blooded animals that have hair or fur and produce milk for their live young. Hyenas are mammals.

nurses (NURS-es): To nurse means to feed offspring with milk from a breast. A female hyena nurses her cubs.

predators (PRED-uh-turs): Predators are animals that eat other animals. Hyenas are fierce predators.

prey (PRAY): Prey are animals that are eaten by other animals. Hyenas hunt and stalk prey in groups.

scavengers (SCAV-en-jers): Scavengers are animals that feed on dead animals. Hyenas are predators and scavengers.

territory (TERR-i-tory): A territory is an animal's home range. A hyena clan's territory can be as large as many miles.

TO LEARN MORE

Books

Grucella, Ethan. *Hyenas*. New York: Gareth Stevens Publishing, 2011.

Quinlan, Julia J. *Hyenas*. New York: PowerKids Press, 2013.

Schuetz, Kari. *Hyenas*. Minneapolis, MN: Bellwether Media, 2012.

Web Sites

Visit our Web site for links about hyenas:

childsworld.com/links

Note to Parents, Teachers, and Librarians: We routinely verify our Web links to make sure they are safe and active sites. So encourage your readers to check them out!

SELECTED BIBLIOGRAPHY

Feldman, David. *What Are Hyenas Laughing At, Anyway?* New York: G.P. Putnam's Sons, 1995.

Grice, Gordon. *The Book of Deadly Animals*. New York: Penguin Books, 2012.

"Hyena." *African Wildlife Foundation*. African Wildlife Foundation, n.d. Web. 7 June 2015.

"Mammals: Spotted Hyena." *San Diego Zoo Animals*. San Diego Zoo Global, 2015. Web. 5 June 2015.

"Spotted Hyena." *National Geographic*. National Geographic, n.d. Web. 7 June 2015.

INDEX

ABOUT THE AUTHOR

Jody Jensen Shaffer is the author of 24 books of fiction and nonfiction for children. She also publishes poetry, stories, and articles in children's magazines. When she is not writing, Jody copy edits for children's publishers. She works from her home in Missouri.